From Pain to Peace

A Grief and Self Discovery Guide

JERI-LYN WASH

From Pain to Peace: A Grief and Self Discovery Guide

Copyright © 2020 Jeri-Lyn Wash.

All rights reserved. This book or any portion thereof may not be reproduced or used in any manner whatsoever without the express written permission of the author except for the use of brief quotations in a book review. Printed in the United States of America Book

First Printing

ISBN 978-1-943284-72-6 pbk

ISBN 978-1-943284-02-3 ebk

A2Z Books Publishing Lithonia, GA 30058 www.A2ZBooksPublishing.net Manufactured in the United States of America A2Z Books Publishing has allowed this work to remain exactly as the Publisher Intended.

Contents

Dedication v

Acknowledgements vii

Introduction 1

Baby, Baby, Baby 5

Heart on Ice 9

Dear Momma 13

I'm Going Down 17

God's Plan 21

Be Careful With Me 29

Who Can I Run To 34

It's Ok To Not Be Ok 39

Don't Judge Me 44

Celebrate 50

All Cried Out 56

After The Pain 59

About The Author 63

About Book 64

Dedication

This book is dedicated to the loving memory of my Grandmother Willie B Wilbon and my beautiful Mother Ella B Wilbon-Wash. In their living, they taught me so many valuable lessons about life, and in their transition, they also taught me so many valuable lessons about grief. This guide will reflect on how I went from Pain to Peace.

Isaiah 40:31

"But those who hope in the Lord will renew their strength. They will soar on wings like eagles; they will run and not grow weary, they will walk and not be faint."

Acknowledgements

I would like to thank my two beautiful children Tajarvis and Nickyla. You are my two biggest blessings. I am nothing without you. I love yall so much

I also want to thank all my siblings, Sondra, Corey, Lisa, Carletta, and Charlene. I love yall more than you will ever know.

To my aunts Ethel and Clemeteen, thanks for always believing in me.

To all my nieces, nephews, and cousins. I love you all, and thanks for always supporting me.

To my friends, I love all of you

Thanks to my whole T.G.I.M family for always pushing me to be great, I love yall.

Shout out and thanks to all my M.O.M. sisters and brothers yall keep me going I love yall.

I want to thank all my supporters.

And last but not least I have to give the biggest thank you to the man who made it all possible. I have to Thank God, Abba, my father, without him, none of this would be possible.

God is Good all the time!

Psalm 107:1

"Give thanks to the Lord, for he is good; his love endures forever."

Jeri's Jewels

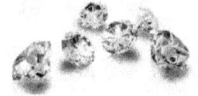

I will be dropping some Jeri's Jewels throughout this book, things that I have gone through, or people I may know who have gone through similar situations. These jewels will show you things to look out for when you're grieving, or you may be associated with someone who is grieving, and they may not even know that they are.

Jeri's Jewels

Grief comes like the seasons, in winter it's cold, and you may feel lonely without your loved ones, remember that every winter has its spring and you'll begin to blossom into happiness. Summer will come around with the sun so hot sometimes it's unbearable to deal with, and you want to stay inside. You're waiting on autumn to cool things down a bit, you may fall a little and begin to feel like the leaves, and that your emotions are scattered everywhere but just know you'll always rise again and find your peace because no season lasts forever.

Proverbs 4:423

"Keep your heart with all diligence, For out of it are the issues of life"

Introduction

What is pain?

Pain is physical suffering or discomfort caused by illness or injury.

It is mental suffering or distress caused by the loss of someone or something.

Jeremiah 29:11

"For I know the plans I have for you," declares the Lord, "plans to prosper you and not to harm you, plans to give you hope and a future."

What is Grief?

Grief is the expected and natural way to respond to an important emotional loss of any kind.

Grief is the unfavorable feeling caused by the ending or change in patterns of behavior.

Grief is also the pain that you feel of deep sorrow, especially caused by someone's death; however, there are so many forms of grief.

John 16:20

"Very truly I tell you, you will weep and mourn while the world rejoices. You will grieve, but your grief will turn to joy."

What is Peace?

Peace is freedom from disturbance; it is a stress-free state; it's a calmness that comes. When you feel at peace with yourself, you are content being the person you are, flaws and all.

Psalm 119:165

"Great peace has those who love your law, and nothing can make them stumble."

Jeri's Jewels

Daily Affirmations

- I am at peace
- I am peaceful
- Peace is my priority
- I am strong
- I am blessed
- I am confident
- I am bold
- I am grateful
- I am healed
- I am healthy
- I am worthy
- I am wealthy
- I am complete

- ♦ I am whole
- ♦ I am fearless
- ♦ I am valuable
- ♦ I am above and not beneath
- ♦ I am the head and not the tail
- ♦ I am a jewel in the lives of all those, that I come in contact with

Philippians 4:13

"I can do all things through Christ Who Strengthens Me."

Jeri's Jewels

Did you know that the first year is normally the hardest year after losing a loved one?

Proverbs 19:21

"Many plans are in a man's heart, but the purpose of Lord will prevail."

Thoughts

Baby, Baby, Baby

❖

Have you ever felt so much pain? The type of pain that seems to all hit you at one time? Well, I have 2016 was one of the most painful years of my life. I didn't see how it could get any worse. I started my year off in 2016, happy! I was happy to have my two beautiful children; I was happy to be engaged and pregnant with a baby on the way. It all seemed so special right? Yea that's what I thought I was sitting on top of the world you couldn't tell me anything, I was finally in a good space in life. Until one day, only a week into the new year that I would suffer a miscarriage at 10 weeks pregnant. (A miscarriage is an early, unintentional end to a pregnancy) I had never experienced a miscarriage before so I didn't know what was to come of it, but it was physically painful, the trauma and changes I witnessed my body go through, and it was also emotionally painful I was an emotional wreck, I didn't quite understand what I was going through, most of the women that I knew who had suffered from miscarriages told me that they were unaffected by it, they said they just moved on, so I thought maybe I would feel the same way. So that's what I thought; yea, right! I don't know about them, but I was affected. It changed me; at that time, I didn't know I was grieving. I didn't even take the time to ask my partner if he was ok seeing it would have been his first child. Most of the time, when a couple suffers a miscarriage, no one thinks about the man and how he may be feeling they only think about the woman as if she is the only one affected, but the truth is they both are affected. I completely dismissed his feelings. A part of me blamed him for the miscarriage; I also blamed myself, I also felt like he blamed me for it as well. I had really changed. I became so angry, I started to nag, we started arguing more, and I did not understand his feelings at all.

I just wanted to block it out and act like it never happened, I never wanted to talk about it, only my close friends and family knew what I was going through and when they would try to ask me questions about it I would snap and tell them I was fine and that they should mind their business. The truth is I wasn't fine, I was grieving and I didn't even know it.

Jeri's Jewels

There is no time clock on healing; there is no arrival or departure time to it, some may say it feels timeless because the hours and days feel long and slow but always remember that after being in the dark midnight hours for so long, early morning brighter days lie ahead and so will your peace and joy.

2 Corinthians 5:7

"For we walk by faith, not by sight."

Thoughts

Heart on Ice

❖

Now we are in June of 2016; something went down in my relationship with my fiance at the time, it was pretty much unrepairable, so I ended the relationship. I am now dealing with a breakup, we all know breakups are never easy! It's like death because now you have to find your new normal without being with that person. I was hurt, but I was trying to remain strong because I was taught always to be strong even if I'm hurting, I was never to let it show, so on the outside I always appeared to be fine I looked good, but on the inside, I was crying and dying I was hurt, and I felt betrayed, so I began to blame myself for another failed relationship, I felt guilty, I became bitter and angry I hated men, and I was mad at the world. I was tired of choosing the wrong men. I was just completely done with men. So whenever a guy would try to talk to me I would be rude and depending on the day or time that you get me wrong they were going to feel my wrath I would curse them clean out without a care in the world, my heart had become ice cold, I had no more love in me, so I just wanted to stop them in their tracks, yes I'm single and leave me alone ughhh. I would call my mother and tell her what I was going through; my mother was a jokester, so she would say stop being so mean, you're going to start looking like an old lady, and she would laugh. My mother always told me I wore my heart on my sleeves; I never wanted to hear that advice. I just didn't even want to be bothered with men at all. I just didn't quite understand why I was going through all of this, how could I lose a baby and a man in one year. I was so confused I began to question God, not knowing at the time I was in so much pain because I was still grieving the loss of the baby, and now the loss of the relationship.

Jeri's Jewels

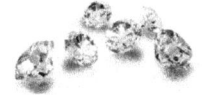

I read an article on Eterneva.com, and it said that a study done by Amerispeak and WebMd says that 57% of people are grieving the loss of someone close to them over the last three years, which means that every other person you see is grieving, because grief never really goes away.

Psalm 29:11

" The Lord will give strength to his people; the Lord will bless his people with peace."

Thoughts

Dear Momma

The end of the year is approaching, and I can't wait for 2016 to be over already. It's just been way too stressful for me. So now, it's November of 2016 when my five siblings and I find out that our mother has been diagnosed with Congestive Heart Failure and that she needed to have an emergency heart surgery. (my mother feared surgery) It was the day before Thanksgiving at 3 am when I got an alarming phone call from my big sister Lisa telling me that our mother did not make it through the surgery because her lungs did not recover. The feeling that I felt was indescribable, and I could have literally passed out, I couldn't breathe. I had to catch my breath because I thought I was going to die right there at that moment, I was devastated, I was shocked, I was crushed, I was a complete wreck, my heart was shattered. There are not enough words to describe how I felt. I felt like my world had just ended at the age of 32. I was now motherless. I had always felt like I was fatherless because I never really had a father, so I always considered my mother as my mother and my father. My mother was all I had; being the youngest of 6 children, I was always her baby no matter how old I got. In life, you only get one mother, so I encourage everyone who mother is still living, it doesn't matter your relationship with your mother, rather it's good or bad because no one is perfect, please love and respect her because you only get one, give her all the love, hugs, kisses and roses while she's still here with you. It's important to appreciate all your loved ones while they are still here because once they are gone, you can no longer pick up that phone and call them or stop by their house to visit. As I began to go through the hurt and pain, I'm sitting here thinking Now what? What do I do now? Why am I still here? I had so many questions. I had now lost my faith; why would God put me through all of this in one year. When my Grandmother passed away in 2014, I saw how it affected my mother and her health. My mother was never the same after losing her mother. I hated 2016 It was the worst Year of my life, how could one person experience so much pain in one year. Why me? Why? Why? Why? I just didn't understand it. At that point, I felt so lost I didn't know what to do or where to turn. It was such a pivotal moment in my life, and I felt like no one understood me, and what I was going through, I knew it was going to be forever changed.

Jeri's Jewels

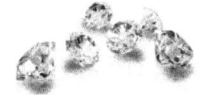

Stages of Grief

- ◆ Isolation
- ◆ Shock
- ◆ Denial
- ◆ Anger
- ◆ Depression
- ◆ Bargaining
- ◆ Acceptance
- ◆ Pain
- ◆ Guilt

Most people who are grieving probably won't experience all the stages, or it will not be in the same order listed. I personally experienced them all. You may also deal with regrets, you know, the what if's and I should have done this, and I should've done that. Each grieving experience in life will affect you differently; it depends on the relationship you had with the person or whatever you may be grieving from, if you were really close to them or if you were their caregiver, all of this plays a part on how you may grieve.

Psalm 48:14

"For this God is our God forever and ever, he will be our guide even to the end."

Thoughts

I'm Going Down

I fell into a deep dark depression, and I became numb to life. I started slacking at work, to the point that they called me into a meeting, and my boss told me to get myself together because my job was on the line. They told me to put my big girl panties on and get it together. It had only been 2 months since my mother died. I couldn't believe that people were so insensitive, but then again, I could because they didn't care about me. All they cared about was me getting the job done. When I walked out of that meeting I felt so defeated all my confidence was gone I really didn't know who I had become, I was so numb and lost that I didn't even defend myself because If I would have I probably would have lost my job that day because I was so furious that I would have snapped and it would not have been pretty. I didn't understand why I was so different. I remember my best friend asked me to go to Orlando with her for some type of girls trip with her new friends. It was only 3 months after losing my mother, I said to myself, is she serious. I sent her a 3 page text telling her about herself. I told her she wasn't a good friend, and how dare she think I want to be having fun, and I just lost my mother. She called me and told me I hurt her feelings, and she was sorry, I didn't want to hear it.

I was completely dismissive of her feelings. The truth is she wasn't a bad friend I was simply grieving, and I didn't even know it, I had completely changed. I was even failing as a mother; everyday, I would just go home, get in bed to sleep, and cry. I wasn't even eating, and I was just wasting away. My sleeping patterns were off. I was waking up every morning at 3 am like clockwork. It wasn't until one day my daughter Nickyla who was 7 years old at the time, came into my room, and she yelled, mommy get up! Get up out of this bed! I set up and looked at her, like little girl, if you don't go sit your butt down somewhere. But I didn't say anything because she spoke with so much authority, she told me to get up because grandma would not want you sleeping and crying everyday all day, grandma would want you to live, so get up and get yourself together. I felt chills all over my body because I knew that was God speaking through my 7 year old daughter.

Jeri's Jewels

<u>Non physical causes of Grief</u>

♦ Loss of Faith (I know a woman who lost her mother to a brutal death, and she shared with me that she had lost her faith in God for a period of time.)

♦ Loss of Fertility (I read a story of a woman who suffered 8 miscarriages, and she grieved the thought of never being able to have a baby and carry to its full term truly.)

♦ Loss of Trust (I know a man who lost all trust in women because of a bad relationship, and he grieved that he would never be able to trust women again.)

♦ Loss of Control (I know a person who was in a long term unhealthy relationship that ended, and they grieved that they lost all control and power over the person once it was really over.)

Nehemiah 8:10

"Do not sorrow, for the joy of the Lord is your strength."

Thoughts

God's Plan

I began to pray and have daily conversations with God. I began to ask God what is my purpose; why am I here, what should I be doing with my life. When I began to know who my father was in heaven and how he has always been with me, he gave me the grace and mercy to get through all of my pain and struggles. I began to understand that God is a mother to the motherless and a father to the fatherless. It was April of 2017 only two weeks before Mother's Day, I was sitting in my car on my lunch break, and I started to think about what do people who have lost their mothers do for mother's day, and all I could hear was have a brunch. I had a friend give me some pointers on how to put the event together. I went home, and I prayed. I asked God to give me a name of the event. It was 3 am when I woke up, all I could hear was Missing Our Mothers. I jumped up and wrote it down. This was when it all began in May 2017. Missing Our Mothers was birthed only six months after my mother made her transition to be with the Lord. I knew now that I had to accept the fact that I had lost my mother truly, and I needed to begin to heal. So I had the first annual Missing Our Mother's Day Brunch. Missing Our Mothers is an organization/support group and our mission is to uplift and inspire people who have lost their mothers or mother figures in a time of need. I now knew that I was not alone and that there were others that shared the same pain. God began to download things for me, different ideas. So I began to visit a few churches, and one night a friend of mine sent me an invitation to visit her church for family and friends day, so I decided to visit her church, The Gathering International Ministry. It was a nice experience, so I visited for about 8 months before I decided to join, when I joined I gained a whole spiritual family at T.G.I.M. God began to push me to open my eyes and allowed me to discover gifts that I was letting lay dormant for years. In just 2 years, I became a Minister at T.G.I.M. I always thank God because I understand that Missing Our Mothers is not about me, it is to help heal others, the truth is our purpose is never about us. We all have a purpose in life, and it is to serve others. I started reading more and taking classes and got some certifications to learn more about grief and bereavement and ways to deal with it. I wanted to be able to identify when someone was going through it. There are so many reasons and things that people grieve from that you may have no clue about because it's not only by losing a loved one to death.

Jeri's Jewels

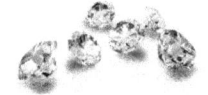

Some causes of Grief

- Death of a loved one (When my mother lost her mother in 2014 it caused her to grieve, it changed her, her health started declining causing her to have heart problems, leading her to make her transition in 2016.)

- Death of a pet (I had a coworker who dog died, and she grieved as if she lost a human family member, she loved her dog, and she told me that she felt empty without her dog because he was in her family for 15 years.)

- Suicide loss (When my friend cousin committed suicide she was so hurt and in denial that he had really taken his own life.)

- Health problems (My friend father was diagnosed with heart disease, and she told me that she noticed a change in him once he was diagnosed, he became very sad, and in denial, he started trying to get everything right with everyone around him because he was grieving the fact that he had a terminal illness, soon after he passed away.)

- Divorce/ending of Relationships/Situationships (My friend once told me that her divorce felt like a death and that someone had knocked the wind out of her.)

- Ending addictions (Drugs, gambling, alcohol, sex, etc. I had an ex who had a gambling addiction and when I found out about it; it really bothered me and put a strain on our relationship, it was really hard for him to stop he was in denial of the damage it was causing, it made him angry, agitated and he began to feel depressed when he decided to stopped.)

- Loss of a job (I have a family member who had lost her job, and she grieved because she was out of work for 2 years and she had children to take care of without help from the children's father she began to isolate herself while dealing with depression.)

- Moving to another state or home (I have a family member that moved to another state with her boyfriend, and she used to grieve the fact that she couldn't be around her family and friends all the time and she was sad that she was missing out on family gatherings and she became very homesick at one point.)

- Starting a new school (My son moved out of town with his dad for 3 years, and when he moved back with me at the age of 16 he grieved the fact of leaving his high school where he had grew in popularity playing football with his friends, only to have to start a new High School that he knew no one at, he became very distant, sad and angry.)

- Retirement (I know an older woman who retired from being on her job for 25 years, she grieved that she would be bored and lonely she became depressed, and eventually she started working a part time job to keep herself busy.)

- Legal problems (I have a guy friend that was put on child support, and he grieved the fact of having to go back in forth to court with the mother of his child to fight for his rights as a father.)

- Prison/Jail (Prisoners themselves go through stages of grief, anger, denial, bargaining, depression, and acceptance, but it also affects the family members who they have left behind; it causes a huge emotional impact on the loved ones. I know a guy who went to prison at a young age, and he ended up doing many years in prison he said one of hardest things for him was leaving his mother because now his mother had to adjust her life to not seeing her baby boy in the house on the daily basis because he was in prison and the fact that they were not able to communicate on their own terms killed his spirit because they were only able to hear each other's voice once or twice a day and having to wait for visits to see each other.)

- Domestic Violence (People who have been involved in domestic violence relationships also grieve and go through stages of grief. I once was in a physical, mental, and emotionally abusive relationship for 5 years, and I was stalked for 6 months when I decided to leave that relationship. I wore many bruises and black eyes while being in that relationship, I had become guilty and blamed myself for what I was going through, I was numb and angry, I remember isolating myself from my friends and family because I was in denial and ashamed of what I was going through.)

- Sexual Assault (People who have been sexually assaulted also goes through stages of grief; they develop fear and anxiety; they may sometimes feel guilty and ashamed of what happened. I know a woman who was raped at 13, and it changed her view on men for along time she was angry she grew not trusting anyone she dealt with depression for years.)

- Abandonment (It's like a form of anxiety it can make someone feel hopeless and depressed and angry, causing them to grieve, making them feel rejection, pain, and guilt; it often begins in childhood. I know a young lady who mother and father left her at a young age causing her to be in and out of foster care, and group homes and some of the stories she has shared with me was absolutely horrible, her experiences caused her always to be angry and fearful she always feared that someone would reject her and leave her causing her never to want to trust anyone and it always affected her relationships.)

You see people grieve from so many different causes and everyone handles it their own way, some people may be grieving, and they have no clue that they are, but we all have been affected by something that has caused us to grieve, it's always important to have a strong prayer life because it helps us however I feel like God made Doctors, Therapists, Counselors and other professionals for a reason. If you need professional help, it's ok to seek it.

Psalm 147:3

"He heals the brokenhearted and binds up their wounds."

Thoughts

Jeri's Jewels

General reactions of Grief

- Fatigue and exhaustion (I found myself always tired and sleeping, not really having energy to do much.)

- Changes in your eating habits (I just wouldn't eat some days at all, it's like my appetite was completely gone.)

- Sleep disturbance (I was waking up every morning at 3 am for 3 years straight completely throwing off my sleep.)

- Weight change (I lost a lot of weight due to not eating and being depressed.)

- Roller coaster of emotions (My emotions was always up and down, crying some days all day but then I had days when I was ok.)

Psalm 34:18

"The Lord is close to the broken hearted and saves those who are crushed in spirit."

Be Careful With Me

When a person is grieving, you have to be mindful of the things you say, you may think that you are comforting them, but in their mind, you may have just really upset them. I remember one time a guy called me one day, and I was a little down that day, so he asked me what was wrong, and I said you know it's only been a month since my mom passed. I'm just not happy right now. His exact words to me were damn you ain't over that yet, I couldn't believe what I just heard. I got so angry that I cursed him out so badly. I hung up the phone, blocked him, and let's just say I never spoke to him again. What he said to me was rude and insensitive. The truth is he probably didn't know that I was grieving or even what grieving was most people don't really know what to say or how to say it, but because I was grieving it caused me to react the way I did. These are a few things that a grieving person may not want to hear.

Jeri's Jewels

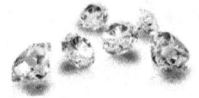

Things you shouldn't say to a grieving person

- Don't feel bad; they are no longer suffering (No one wants to hear that when they just loss a loved one, they haven't even processed the loss yet.)

- It was just an animal (That is not nice to say, and it's not helpful, people love their pets just like they are family.)

- I know how you feel (People don't want to hear that especially when you have not experienced that certain type of loss.)

- You shouldn't be feeling that way still (It's not nice to say and know one should try and rush you in your grieving process.)

- Stay strong (Telling a person to stay strong makes them feel like it's not ok to grieve and that they should just keep it moving.)

- You're still young; you can still have other children (A person does not want to hear that when they have just lost a child, it makes them feel like your saying it's no big deal that they lost a child.)

1 Peter 5:7

"Give all your worries to him, because he cares for you."

Thoughts

Jeri's Jewels

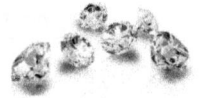

There is no expiration date on grieving because it will never get too old or spoil; some days, it may be good as a piece of cake freshly baked, while other days, it may be as bad as a glass of spoiled milk.

Philippians 4:6

" Be anxious for nothing, but in everything by prayer and supplications, with thanksgiving let your request be made known to God."

Jeri's Jewels

You don't have to try and act like you're some kind of superhuman hero when you're probably feeling like the weight of the world is on your shoulders while you're grieving so you may not want to go to your friends for help and comfort because you would rather keep your feelings bottled inside but always remember this, it's ok to reach out to someone because even Batman needed Robin to help him at times and to keep him grounded. We all need someone we can trust and share our feelings with.

Proverbs 11:25

" The generous soul will be made rich, and he who waters will also be watered himself."

Who Can I Run To

❖

I know sometimes when people are going through it, you may like to keep count on how many people showed up to support you in your time of bereavement and you may be looking for ways to be upset with the world, but support comes in different forms. It's not just people showing up to the funeral or wake because some people really can't stomach those type of ceremonies. And that's ok so let's not be so quick to judge them hopefully they will support you in other ways. I had a friend who didn't come to my mother funeral, and that really hurt me I was really upset I vowed never to be friends with that person again, our friendship was strained for about 2 years because I was so upset I felt like she wasn't there when I needed her, but the reason she didn't make it to the funeral was that she was out of town and didn't make it back in town on time. I have now forgiven her because I understand now, but when I was going through it, I had no understanding at all. When people are grieving they want to hear comforting words, they want to feel like you are sensitive to what they are going through, they need you to listen and have sympathy without judging them or saying that you know how they feel because each person who is grieving have different situations and stories. When I lost my mother, 3 of my friends came over to my house immediately to comfort me. They allowed me to cry on their shoulders and let me vent to them without interrupting me, and I needed that at that time.

Jeri's Jewels

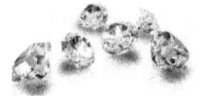

Offer Assistance

- ♦ Child care (If you can maybe offer child sitting, that can be a big help because when a person is in bereavement, it's kind of hard to focus on the children so maybe taking the child/children for a few hours or maybe even a night so that they can focus on the next steps, it really can be a big help.)

- ♦ Groceries (Offering to pick up some groceries for them, because at that time they will probably have a lot of family visiting so they won't have time to do those sort of things.)

- ♦ Arrangements (Ask them if they need any help or suggestions with making arrangements for the funeral.)

John 15:12

" My command is this, love each other as I have loved you."

Jeri's Jewels

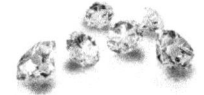

Things You Can Do/Say To A Grieving Person

♦ Give them a hug, and say nothing (Sometimes all a person need is a real genuine hug, no words needed just a hug.)

♦ Say nothing and just be with them (Just sitting with them and simply being there is enough.)

♦ I'm sorry for your loss.

♦ Let them know that you're only a phone call away and that your here for them (Giving them that assurance lets them know you are there for them, is very much needed.)

♦ Let them know that they are in your thoughts and prayers (It's very encouraging to know that someone is praying for you in your time of bereavement.)

It's the smallest and the simplest things that you may not even think matter that will matter the most. It is important just to try to be there for them as much as you can, even if they decline the help they will remember who was there when they went through that hard time, and they will truly appreciate it in the end.

2 Samuel 2:6

"May the Lord now show you kindness and faithfulness, and I too will show you the same favor because you have done this."

It's Ok To Not Be Ok

Don't rush your grieving process. There is no right or wrong way to grieve. You have to roll with the punches day by day. Everyone has their own different experiences when dealing with grief. Just know that it is completely ok to have your down moments and not be ok, you will not be in that space forever that's why you must stay connected with supportive people. Having a strong prayer life and a support system can really make a difference in your grieving process. A support system can include your family, friends, leaders in faith, or a support group.

Jeri's Jewels

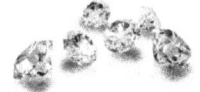

Things to remember when you are not feeling ok

- Let yourself feel (Allow yourself to feel however you feel at that moment rather it's good or bad)

- Remember that you are not a burden (You are not alone you have people who love and care about you)

- Breathe (Take a deep breath and breathe)

- Talk about your feelings (You can not heal what you don't reveal, so it's important to talk about how you're feeling with your support system)

- Slow down (Sometimes we try to keep ourselves so busy that we just go none stop, it's ok to slow down and relax)

Proverbs 3:5

" Trust in the Lord with all your heart, and do not lean on your own understanding."

Thoughts

Jeri's Jewels

Sometimes grief leaves us in such a miserable state that you begin to carry a heavy heart with sadness and pain, and if you don't heal properly, it will begin to be so heavy that no one else can help you carry it because it has weighed you down like a ton of bricks. It's our good memories that are full of love and kindness that gives us hope and lightens our heart with peace.

Proverbs 12:25

"Anxiety in a man's heart weighs it down, But a good word makes it glad."

Thoughts

Don't Judge Me

❖

When most people hear counseling or therapy, they think of it in a negative way; they begin to say things like I don't need to go talk to anybody about what I'm going through. I'm not crazy, yes I am her, and she is me! I was one of the people who thought like that, I felt like I was going to be judged and called crazy for seeking counseling, but I had to build up the courage to do it, and I did it. I seeked one on one counseling and it helped me unpack a lot of baggage that I was carrying for years, and I was just taking it from one situation to the next never truly healing. The truth is I would recommend everyone to seek counseling or therapy after going through any traumatic experience, for example when people get out of a bad relationship you should seek counseling because if you don't heal from what hurt you; you'll end up bleeding on people who didn't cut you. So it's very important for your mental health, therapy can also help you work on your goals, it helps you untangle years of confusion and turmoil; it also helps you change unhealthy patterns. Most people won't seek therapy or join a support group because they think it's weird, and it's very unpopular in some cultures, so a lot of people frown upon it. Having a grief counselor/coach is not a bad thing because it's important to share your grief with people who can relate that way you can work through your emotions in a safe setting. Well let me tell you this, it has helped me tremendously. It allowed me to open up and share with people who were going through the same things as me. I also learned so many alternative therapies so that you are not just sitting in a group circle feeling embarrassed or bored, but ways to make it fun so that you look forward to your next support group meeting.

Jeri's Jewels

Creative Alternative Grief Therapy

- Journaling therapy (I began journaling writing down my feelings and ideas, this is a great form of therapy it's great for mental and emotional clarity.)

- Art therapy/Painting with a Purpose (My sister began painting, and she said it was a good form of therapy because it allows her to express herself on the painting canvas she felt as if she was painting the pain away and relieving stress and putting her mind at ease.)

- Yoga therapy (We have done yoga with our support group while listening to neo soul music as we did different breathing exercises to improve our mental and physical health.)

- Music/Laugh therapy (We have done karaoke with our group, music is a form a therapy as well as laughing, and we laughed, and laughed, laughing is, and will always be, the best form of therapy, laughing is the sound of the soul dancing, it also reduces stress.)

- Retail therapy (Who doesn't like a little shopping? Shopping makes everyone happy, let's just say Marshall's, Ross, the mall and Amazon has definitely been my best friend when I'm in a not so good mood, so it helps you in moments of depression or stress.

Just make sure you place yourself on a budget because you never want to overspend.)

- ♦ Traveling therapy (I have a friend that loves traveling all over the world, she has been to Honduras, Barcelona, Morocco, Greece, and that's not even half of the places she has traveled to, but that's part of her therapy mechanism she said that traveling increases her energy and helps her think better and clearer, and most importantly it gives her positive emotions and makes her happy, and relieves stress.)

- ♦ Massage therapy (I try to get a massage every 3 months because it helps me relax and it reduces stress, and it helps with anxiety and depression you maybe dealing with.)

- ♦ Cooking therapy (I have a friend that loves to cook and try new recipes when she is feeling down and depressed, she said that cooking for others makes her happy and keeps her anxiety down plus it's a creative outlet.)

- ♦ Social circles (We get together once a month, and we go out to lunch or dinner, and we just continue to encourage and support each other, this is also very therapeutic.)

Proverbs 15:22

" Plans fail without advice, but succeed with wise counsel."

Thoughts

Jeri's Jewels

Grief comes in like ocean waves, it goes up and down you may feel like you're drowning some days with the thoughts of not having that person anymore and some days you may feel like you're just floating through life, and then you'll have your days when you have made it to shore, and you have landed at peace.

2 Thessalonians 3:16

"Now may the Lord of peace himself give you peace always in every way. The Lord be with you all."

Celebrate

It's never easy remembering a loved one who has passed, so It's normal to feel sad around all the major holidays, such as Mother's day, Father's day, Christmas, Thanksgiving, their birthday, wedding anniversary, and the anniversary date that the person passed on, another thing is if they passed away from certain causes, like breast cancer and heart disease and more, these moments are hard. It will sometimes put you right back in that grieving place that you have worked so hard to come out of, it may make you feel like it just happened all over again. What I have learned to do is to have gratitude and just be thankful for the time that I was able to share with my loved one it may sound strange, and yes it's always ok to grieve and take your moments to cry, but it is very important to find time to remember and celebrate too. I believe that our loved ones would not want us to be sad and to celebrate those special days in honor of them.

Jeri's Jewels

Ways To Celebrate A Deceased Loved One

♦ Make their favorite dish (For Christmas and Thanksgiving my mother used to make her famous egg pie which is also my favorite, so now I try to make it every year, ummm I haven't quite mastered it yet (ha ha) but I'll get right one day.)

♦ Have a special remembrance dinner (Every year my friend makes a remembrance dinner for her mom and dad, with her close friends and family.)

♦ Find a way to serve (I have a friend who mother passed away from breast cancer and every year she does a bake sale and donates all the proceeds to breast cancer awareness foundation.)

♦ Spend the day doing something they would have enjoyed doing (I like to wear my mother favorite color, and I have a sister that love to visit my mother favorite park in honor of her, but you can do whatever makes you happy that day.)

♦ Have a candlelight or balloon release (You can get together with close friends and family and enjoy this in honor of your loved ones.)

♦ Play their favorite song (one of my mother's favorite song was Butta Love by the group Next.)

- Memorial jewelry (My best friend surprised me with a necklace with my mom name on it, it was such a beautiful gift and a great way to honor my mother.)

- Take flowers to their grave site (I know plenty of people who visit their loved one grave site often and take flowers and balloons.)

- Candles (My mother wishes was to be cremated, so my sister used some of her ashes and got them to put in candles for all 6 siblings, so we all have a candle in honor our mother, she also plans to plant a tree in honor of our mother.)

- Support/Walk for the cause (If your loved one passed away from a certain cause such as breast cancer or heart disease, gun violence, or any type of other cause, try to support and bring awareness to that cause in honor of your loved one.)

- Start a scholarship or foundation to honor them (I started my organization to honor my mother because I was missing her so badly but also to help others. I also have a friend who started a foundation and scholarship in her mother's name to honor her.)

2 Corinthians 5:8

" We are confident, I say, and willing rather to be absent from the body, and to be present with the Lord"

Thoughts

Jeri's Jewels

Did you know that about 2.5 million people die in the United States every year, each leaving an average of five grieving people behind.

Numbers 6:26

"The Lord lift up his countenance upon you, and give you peace."

Thoughts

All Cried Out

❖

You may experience many tears throughout your grieving process, you are probably going to cry so much that you may think you have no more tears left to cry, but our crying is like a cleansing to our soul there's a reason for our tears whether it's happy or sad tears. Tears are the words that our hearts can't communicate. It's very important to know that it's completely normal and it's ok to cry. Crying does not mean that you are weak, it simply means that you have a heart and you are experiencing real human emotions for your loved one, or whatever it is that you are grieving from.

Jeri's Jewels

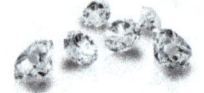

The Tears of Grief

The Tears of Grief
T= To acknowledge the reality of the loss
E= Experience the pain of the loss
A= Accept the new normal without the person
R= Regain your new reality
S= Start to live again

Revelation 21:4

"He will wipe every tear from their eyes. There will be no more death' or mourning or crying or pain, for the old order of things has passed away."

Jeri's Jewels

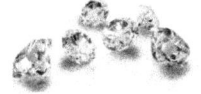

Grief is like a fingerprint; it's unique to each person; it will probably be no one else in the world who will have your same exact grieving experience because not even identical twins have the same set of fingerprints.

Jude 1:2

"May mercy, peace and love be multiplied to you."

After The Pain

After going through the physical pain, the depression, the betrayal, the hurt, and the sadness, that I thought I would never overcome, I had to realize that in life we are going to go through all kinds of things, some good, some bad, moments when you're up and moments when you're down, but we have to understand that all that we go through is a part of life, it's a part of our testimony, and our testimony can help save others. Through all the pain that I experienced and the grief that I had endured, I learned to embrace it, and through it all, I will empower others to find peace in situations that may seem painful at the time. If you look back over your past and think about the painful things you have been through it all has a purpose to it, our pain helps us discover our strength, our pain matures us, pain is the price for a greater reward and our pain pushes us into our purpose and peace. But it's the peace that we experience with our faith in God that will surpass any temporary peace that the world can give you, and it can ease your deepest fears and calm your broken heart.

FROM PAIN TO PEACE

John 14:27

Peace I leave with you; my peace I give to you.
Not as the world gives do I give to you. Let not your hearts be troubled, neither let them be afraid."

Jeri's Jewels

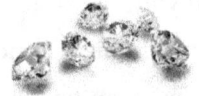

Going through the pain is like a journey, because you are traveling through your emotions and your moods always seem to change one stop at a time. The first stop you may be happy and full of excitement and then the next stop on the journey you may be lonely, and heart broken but then you feel like you're on a new path to joy when you bump into fear; you may feel afraid of what's next. Throughout all the long roads on this journey the best feeling is when you have arrived at peace.

- ◆ P - Patience for the journey
- ◆ E - Embrace the journey
- ◆ A - Adjust to the journey
- ◆ C - Courage for the journey
- ◆ E - Encourage others on the journey

Luke 1:79

" To give light to those who sit in darkness and the shadow of death, to guide our feet into the way of peace"

About The Author

Jeri-Lyn Wash was born March 17,1984 in Gary, Indiana; she is the youngest of six siblings; in 1998 at the tender age of 13, she moved to Fort Lauderdale Florida with her mother and big sister. She has two wonderful children, a son and daughter who she loves and adores. Jeri is a mother, a sister, a cousin, an aunt, a friend, a mentor, a minister, and so much more, she is simply Just Jeri. Jeri began journaling after her mom passed away in 2016. When she began developing her relationship with God, healing became a part of her life. She is the President and Founder of an organization called Missing Our Mothers Inc. Her purpose in life is to encourage, heal, and uplift others from pain to peace.

https://www.missingourmothers.org/

Psalm 139:14

"I praise you because I am fearfully and wonderfully made; your works are wonderful; I know that full well."

About Book

This book is a guide to show you how to overcome painful situations and how to begin to heal. This guide will open your eyes to grief and the many causes and stages of it. Jeri will drop jewels throughout the book to encourage you as well as educate you.

Romans 8:18

"I am sure what we are suffering now cannot compare with the glory that will be shown to us."

Interested in Writing and or Publishing a Book?
Visit www.a2zbookspublishing.net